Happy
Sloth Day!

April Pulley Sayre with Jeff Sayre

Beach Lane Books • New York London Toronto Sydney New Delhi

After a rainy,
drizzly night,
a sloth feels cool.
It needs to climb.

When you live
inside your laundry,
morning's

d_ri_p-d_ry

time.

Sloth Cool

Sloths are cool. A three-toed sloth's average body temperature is 91 degrees Fahrenheit—a human's is 97.9. Sloths are energy savers. Their bodies do not spend much energy heating up or staying at a steady temperature. As a result, a sloth does not require high-energy fuels such as meat or fruit. A sloth eats low-calorie leaves. The downside of this low-temperature life is that sloths chill easily. If a sloth gets really cold, the leaf-digesting bacteria inside its stomach stop working. Fortunately, sloths live in tropical forests that tend to be warm year-round.

A little breeze on the belly.

A little sun on the side.

Time crawls. The sloth travels.

Arms stretch wide.

Rain Forest Camouflage

Sloths have natural camouflage. Their fur is mostly a treelike gray or black. Each hair has tiny cracks that wick in water. Green algae, fungi, and other microbes grow in these moist cracks. The algae tint a sloth's fur green, which helps it match a tree even better.

Male brown-throated sloths, a species of three-toed sloths, have a bright orange-yellow back patch. The reason for these bright patches is still a mystery.

A tree is sloth salad.

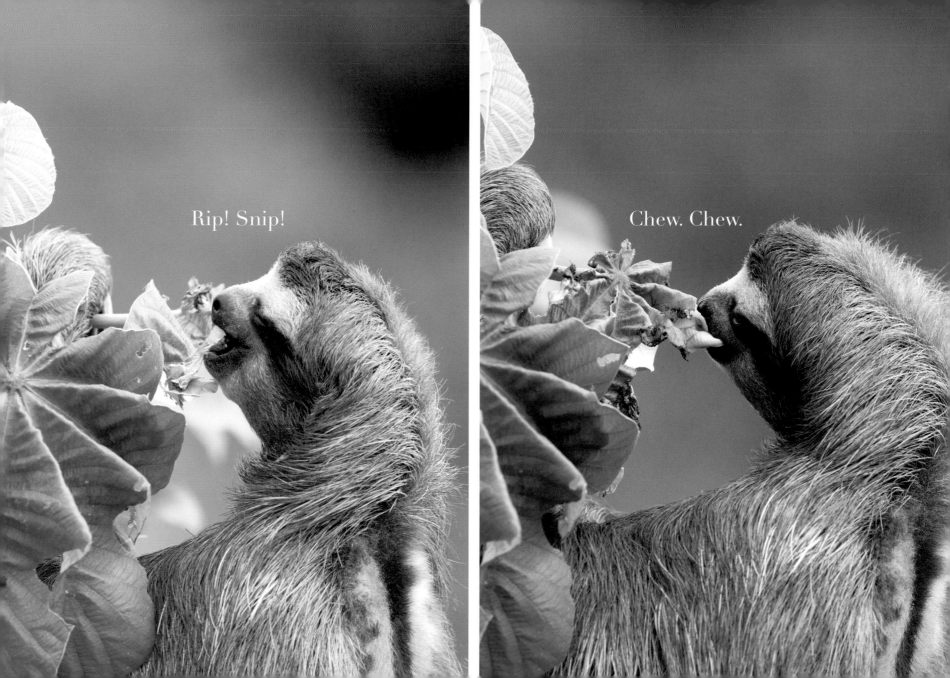

Rip! Snip!

Chew. Chew.

Head turn.

Slowwwwly

scan.

What's the treetop view?

The Canopy View

Almost all mammals, from gerbils to giraffes to humans, have seven neck vertebrae. Sloths have eight to ten neck vertebrae. Thanks to these neck bones, a sloth can turn its head 270 degrees to view the canopy layer. This treetop forest layer is full of activity. Woodpeckers tap on tree trunks to find grubs. Hummingbirds sip nectar from flowers. Iguanas gobble leaves. A cuckoo thrashes a caterpillar against a branch to remove its spines before eating it.

Sloths may seem to live in a big salad—the forest. Alas, not every leaf is tasty or healthy. Wild plants often contain toxins, which help plants to defend against leaf eaters. Sloths sniff a tree's leaves before eating them. Smell tells them about the chemistry of a leaf—whether or not it is safe to eat. A baby sloth learns from its mother which tree leaves are good to eat.

The canopy is busy.

Hammer.

Hover.

Crunch.

Catch.

Pause.

Time for claws.

Elbow up . . .

back

scratch!

Fingers, Toes, and Claws

True claws, like those of cats and dogs, are made mostly of keratin, the same material as your fingernails. But a sloth's "claws" are made mostly of its finger bones, covered with only a thin bit of keratin. Its back feet have hooks made from its toe bones, covered with keratin too.

Both three-toed and two-toed sloths have three clawlike toes on their back feet. It is their front fingers that differ in number. Three-toed sloths have three clawlike fingers. Two-toed sloths have two clawlike fingers. No wonder sloth researcher Dr. Rebecca Cliffe prefers to call them two- and three-*fingered* sloths instead.

It's actually easier to tell these sloths apart by their face patterns. Three-toed sloths have masklike face patterns, with streaks reaching from their eyes back toward their ears. Two-toed sloths have brown circles around their eyes, but no masklike streaks.

Swish, swish!
Howlers hop.
Monkeys shake
the leafy ocean.

Branches rise and fall.

The sloth sways with the motion.

Monkey versus Sloth

Three-toed sloths and howler monkeys are mammals. Both kinds of mammals eat leaves. Both have tails. But their bodies handle treetop life in different ways. A howler monkey's tail is a counterbalance—distributing weight for tree-trunk travel. Its tail is also prehensile—muscular enough to grasp a branch as an anchor or brace. A three-toed sloth's tail is short and stubby. It can't counterbalance or wrap around a tree limb. But it does help a sloth balance on a branch or wedge itself into the crotch of a tree.

Monkeys have strong muscles to press, push, and brace themselves. They can leap. They can walk along the tops of branches. Monkeys can stand on all fours, or even on two legs for short periods.

Sloths cannot leap or stand up on their hind legs. They have less muscle than monkeys do. Yet sloths are still strong—just in a different way. Sloth muscles have "slow twitch" muscle fibers, which are better for holding on and shifting than for pushing and bouncing. They move along, suspended beneath the branch instead of on top of it. These lean muscles are also good for swimming.

Such busy knees,
tails, toes!

Press.

Perch.

Anchor.

Wrap.

A sun-warmed sloth settles
for a sleepy-sloth nap.

Not Always Sleepy

People used to think that sloths were very sleepy and slept a lot more than humans. But they assumed this based on studies of sloths in zoos. Researcher Bryson Voirin decided to study sloth sleep in the wild. He fitted wild sloths with small caps that contain sensors to detect brain waves that indicate sleep. Voirin's work shows that every twenty-four hours, sloths spend nine to ten hours sleeping. That's not much more sleep than human teenagers need. Teenagers need an estimated eight to ten hours out of every twenty-four. Koalas often sleep for twenty hours, so they win the sleepy prize.

No one quiets.
Howlers hurry.
They bound
and bend
and brace.

A paw,
a jaw,
teeth saw. . . .

Umbrella

leaves,

meet

face!

The Umbrella-Leafed Tree

Cecropia trees have umbrella-shaped leaves and finger-shaped fruit. These trees are some of the first trees to grow along forest edges or light gaps—areas where trees fall and let light onto the forest floor. Three-toed sloths eat the leaves of many kinds of trees. But sloths are the most visible—and therefore most often photographed—in the wide-open branches of the Cecropia trees.

Bite by bite,
the day passes.
An afternoon
is well spent

letting leaves

in a tummy

ferment.

Like a Cow in a Tree

A sloth is a bit like a cow in a tree. Inside sloth and cow stomachs are bacteria that help break down leaves through a process called fermentation. Both cows and sloths have four stomach chambers. Cows and sloths move slowly and take their time digesting food.

Cows and sloths, when they digest leaves, produce gas. This gas comes out of a cow's rear as flatulence (farts). Sloths, instead, absorb the gas into their bloodstream. The gas is then expelled through their lungs and out of their mouth.

Almost a third of a sloth's body is stomach—and that tummy is just about full of leaves all the time. An individual leaf may spend anywhere from one week to seven weeks inside a sloth before its remains are deposited in droppings. Another leaf eater, the howler monkey, digests leaves much more quickly. By digesting quickly, howlers gain additional energy and can be more active than sloths.

Then, suddenly,
creatures scatter.
A sloth can't scurry.
But it can freeze.

Is a harpy eagle hunting?

No.

Hawks spiral

above the trees.

Sloth Safety

Sloths stay safe mostly by avoiding being seen. They are slow moving, quiet, and not very smelly. Their greenish-gray fur is good camouflage. Harpy eagles hunt and eat sloths, but smaller birds of prey, such as hawks, do not.

Sloths face their biggest dangers on the ground when they descend to bury their droppings or to cross to another tree. On the ground, jaguars may prey on them. Or a sloth may need to cross a busy road. Sloths cannot do a push-up, so they cannot lift their tummy and crawl. Sloths can only reach out, dig their claws in the dirt, and pull their body along. Some people stop to help sloths cross the road or put up "sloth crossing" signs asking motorists to slow down. When the Amazon river floods, sloths do not have to descend and crawl from tree to tree. They can swim instead!

They migrate past.

All is safe.

Climb down.

Curl up.

Out of view.

Is this
The End?
Not by a stretch.
Here comes the
nighttime crew!

The Changing of the Sloths

A sloth's sleep pattern is not set in stone. Sloths, like many other mammals, can vary their sleep pattern according to neighborhood conditions. In mainland Panama, late afternoon and evening is the time for the changing of the sloths. Here, three-toed sloths are primarily diurnal—active during the day. Two-toed sloths are nocturnal—mostly active at night.

Two-toed sloths spend the day tucked in a tangle of vines, out of view. Then they emerge in the evening to forage and dine on tree leaves. That's just about when the three-toed sloths are ready to snooze. Like the daytime forest, the nighttime forest is busy. Woolly opossums, night monkeys, kinkajous, bats, moths, and other creatures are out feeding too.

A mommy hammock climbs.

Furry arms hold her tight.

As three-toed day
turns into
two-toed night.

Sloth Science

In a world of noisy, speedy, flapping, bouncing animals, does a slowish, greenish, leaf-eating mammal matter? Yes. The more scientists study sloths, the more they find these mammals have important connections to other animals, plants, and even fungi.

Sloths and Their Trees

Sloth droppings help fertilize the trees they inhabit. Every week or so, three-toed sloths climb down from their trees. They dig a hole, defecate (produce droppings), and try to cover them up. Instead of using their hind feet to scratch dirt over the buried droppings as cats do, sloths do a sort of poop-dance. They waggle their posterior to dig a shallow hole in the ground, then poop, then waggle a bit more to push leaves over the droppings. Two-toed sloths do not have a tail like three-toed sloths do, so their droppings are not as well covered.

Moths and Sloths

Sloth moths are small, triangular, white or brown-and-cream-striped moths that sharp-eyed readers might spot on sloths in this book. While a sloth is doing its business, sloth moths—at least five species—crawl down off the sloth and lay their eggs on the sloth droppings. The eggs hatch, and caterpillars emerge in a pile of leafy sloth droppings, which serve as caterpillar food. After a caterpillar transforms into a winged moth, it flies up into the canopy until it finds the right kind of sloth. It crawls on the sloth's fur until the sloth descends from the tree to defecate. The process begins again.

Giant Sloths and Joshua Trees

Today's sloths are related to giant ground sloths that once lived in North and South America. Those sloths were 15 feet (4.6 meters) tall and weighed almost 6,000 pounds (2,722 kilograms)—as much as an African elephant. Some giant sloths ate fruit from Joshua trees—yes, the same kind that live in Joshua Tree National Park. The sloths helped Joshua Trees spread to new areas. The sloths wandered, and Joshua Tree seeds sprouted in their droppings.

Giant Sloths and Armadillos

Sloths not only affect other plants and creatures, they can impact the landscape. For years, people puzzled over strange caves in Brazil. They did not look like caves made by lava, rain, or underground rivers. Researcher Renato Pereira Lopes and his team examined deep grooves on the cave walls. The grooves matched up with one thing: giant ground-sloth claws! Apparently, the huge animals dug lots of these paleoburrows ten thousand years ago. What other animals might have lived in these caves and helped dig them? Ancient armadillos!

Saving Sloths

Sloths may be slow moving, but many sloth species are very successful. In Panama, sloths are one of the most common large wild mammals. The main threat to sloths is habitat loss—the destruction of rain forests and dry forests. These forests are cleared for lumber, for housing, for raising cattle, and for growing soybeans, palm oil, and cotton. Sloths also die during capture and transport for the pet trade and for people in cities who want photos taken with sloths. (Sloths make terrible pets. They have sensitive stomachs, require a lot of expensive veterinary care, and often die in captivity.) For information on helping sloths, including adopt-a-sloth programs, see the Sloth Conservation Foundation, slothconservation.org.

Study the Sloth

Sloths are so popular in books and movies that you might think scientists know everything about them. But they do not. For starters, a big, furry sloth, crawling with moths and beetles and coated with algae and fungi, is a roving ball of habitat for small creatures. Microbiologist Dr. Sarah Higginbotham surveyed the bacteria and fungi on sloth fur and found that many strains showed promise in fighting cancer, malaria, and other diseases. (By the way, the studies were on fur gathered by researcher Bryson Voirin, the scientist who studied sloth sleep. Scientists not only work in teams, they often help each other out when they can. Perhaps someday you will decode some more sloth science and help not only sloths, but also humans!)

Photo and Forest Details

Six sloth species inhabit the world's forests. The ones in this book are the brown-throated sloth *(Bradypus variegatus)*, which is a type of three-toed sloth, and the Hoffman's sloth *(Choloepus hoffmanni)*, a type of two-toed sloth. All the animals in this book were photographed in the wild. For photo identification of them, visit AprilSayre.com.

"Rain forest" is a casual term people use for tropical forests where it rains a lot. But scientists have many different classifications of tropical forests. Some of these forests have wet seasons and dry seasons, as does Soberanía National Park, Panama, where this book was photographed. Most of this book was photographed from Panama's Canopy Tower (canopytower.com), an ecolodge at eye level with the canopy creatures, 50 feet (15 meters) off the ground. The harpy eagle was photographed by Carlos Bethancourt on expedition from the Canopy Camp in the Darién Province.

Resources for More Leisurely Chewing

Cliffe, Rebecca, and Suzi Eszterhas. *Sloths: Life in the Slow Lane*. Preston, Lancashire, UK: The Sloth Conservation Foundation, 2017. A fantastic in-depth biology/photo book by a scientist.

Kricher, John. *The New Neotropical Companion*. Princeton, NJ: Princeton University Press, 2017. Deep ecology about forests that sloths inhabit.

Sayre, April Pulley, and Kelly Murphy. *The Slowest Book Ever*. Honesdale, PA: Boyds Mills Press, 2016. A book for moving on from sloths to pondering other slow science and humor.

Wainwright, Mark. *The Mammals of Costa Rica: A Natural History and Field Guide*. Ithaca, NY: Cornell University Press, 2007. Top-notch introduction to sloths, monkeys, and tropical forests.

With love and gratitude to Raúl Arias de Para, Denise Barakat de Arias, Carlos and Evelyn Bethancourt, and all the Canopy Family

Acknowledgments

Jeff and I photographed this book in the country of Panama near the Canopy Tower and Canopy Lodge. We have traveled with the Canopy Family eight times over the last twenty years. We treasure the friendship and hospitality of its visionary founder and conservationist, Raúl Arias de Para. Our dear friend Carlos Bethancourt, who is a renowned nature guide and businessman, helped bring us some of the best nature experiences of our lives. We honor the wisdom passed down from his grandmother, Graciela. Special thanks to Danilo Rodriguez Sr. and Felipe Rodriguez. Thank you also to sloth researcher Dr. Rebecca Cliffe of Swansea University for scientific review. For sloth fans who want to dive deeper, we highly recommend her book, *Sloths: Life in the Slow Lane*, photographed by Suzi Eszterhas, and Cliffe's website, slothconservation.org.

BEACH LANE BOOKS

An imprint of Simon & Schuster Children's Publishing Division • 1230 Avenue of the Americas, New York, New York 10020 • © 2022 by April Pulley Sayre • Book design by Rebecca Syracuse © 2022 by Simon & Schuster, Inc. • All rights reserved, including the right of reproduction in whole or in part in any form. • BEACH LANE BOOKS and colophon are trademarks of Simon & Schuster, Inc. • For information about special discounts for bulk purchases, please contact Simon & Schuster Special Sales at 1-866-506-1949 or business@simonandschuster.com. • The Simon & Schuster Speakers Bureau can bring authors to your live event. For more information or to book an event, contact the Simon & Schuster Speakers Bureau at 1-866-248-3049 or visit our website at www.simonspeakers.com. • The text for this book was set in A Font with Serifs. • Manufactured in China • 1221 SCP • First Edition • 10 9 8 7 6 5 4 3 2 1 • Library of Congress Cataloging-in-Publication Data • Names: Sayre, April Pulley, author. | Sayre, Jeff, 1963– author. • Title: Happy sloth day! / April Pulley Sayre with Jeff Sayre. • Description: First edition. | New York : Beach Lane Books, [2022] | Includes bibliographical references. | Audience: Ages 0–8 | Audience: Grades 2–3 | Summary: "Take a sloth's-eye view of the world in this beautiful and informative photographic picture book. Young readers will see where sloths live, what they eat, how they hide from predators, and much more. They'll learn about the creatures that interact with and depend on sloths in the interconnected and fragile tropical forest ecosystem"—Provided by publisher. • Identifiers: LCCN 2021003785 (print) | LCCN 2021003786 (ebook) | ISBN 9781534453739 (hardcover) | ISBN 9781534453746 (ebook) • Subjects: LCSH: Sloths—Juvenile literature. • Classification: LCC QL737.E2 S29 2022 (print) | LCC QL737.E2 (ebook) | DDC 599.3/13—dc23 • LC record available at https://lccn.loc.gov/2021003785 • LC ebook record available at https://lccn.loc.gov/2021003786